# How to Write a Story
## GRADES 4-6

Editorial Development: Marilyn Evans
Jo Ellen Moore
Leslie Sorg
Copy Editing: Cathy Harber
Cover: Liliana Potigian
Illustration: Don Robison
Art Direction: Marcia Smith
Design/Production: Jia-Fang Eubanks
Morgan Kashata

EMC 794

**Evan-Moor®**

Visit
*teaching-standards.com*
to view a correlation
of this book.
This is a free service.

**Correlated to
Current Standards**

CPSIA: McNaughton & Gunn, Saline, MI USA [11/2021]

# Contents

# What's Inside

*How to Write a Story* provides older students with everything they need to learn to write creative, interesting short stories. This book is full of directions, guides, and templates to aid your instruction.

## Part I: Learn the Parts of a Story

In this section, students learn to identify and develop characters, settings, plots, and conclusions of stories. Activities are presented in a scaffolded format; choose those most appropriate for your students. Activities include identifying the parts of a story in literature, describing and illustrating the parts of a story, and writing their own story parts. At the end of this section, students combine what they have learned and created to write an original story.

## Part II: Write a Story Step by Step

Forms are provided to guide students to write a story step by step. From story plan sheets and graphic organizers to a conclusion page, this section makes your job easier!

## Part III: Additional Story-Planning Forms

Forms for an outline, a question and answer list, and a story web provide even more ways for students to plan stories.

## Part IV: Write in Different Genres

Once students have mastered the parts of a story and the steps for writing a story, challenge them to write in specific genres! Teaching suggestions and guided directions for students are included for realistic fiction, historical fiction, mystery, adventure, fantasy, and science fiction stories.

## Part V: Presentation

Encourage students' creativity with reproducible templates to create and illustrate final copies of stories.

## Part VI: Writing and Publishing Centers

### Writing Center

The Writing Center contains materials to encourage independent story writing. Story prompt cards, character and setting lists, and charts for writing in specific genres will cure even the most difficult case of writer's block.

### Publishing Center

Older students can publish their own stories with the help of this center. Simply provide various materials for the illustrations and covers, as well as the final copy templates in this book.

# Trait-Based Writing

*How to Write a Story* fits perfectly if you're using trait-based writing! When your students use this book, they develop these skills:

## Conventions

- Spelling
- Possessives
- Complete sentences
- End punctuation
- Capitalization
- Indenting paragraphs
- Commas and quotation marks in dialogue

## Voice

- Examining different writing styles
- Choosing a voice to match your purpose
- Writing from different points of view
- Using different voices for different purposes
- Developing your own voice

## Ideas

- Choosing a strong idea
- Developing character, setting, and plot ideas
- Elaborating on ideas and details
- Maintaining focus

## Word Choice

- Writing about action
- Using descriptive language
- Choosing words for your audience
- Getting the reader's attention

## Sentence Fluency

- Beginning sentences in different ways
- Combining sentences
- Writing a smooth paragraph

## Organization

- Sequencing
- Developing a complete story
- Grouping together ideas and details

Use this scoring rubric, based on the Six-Traits writing model, to assess your students' stories.

# Scoring Rubric

Student's Name _____

| | 1 | 2 | 3 | 4 | Score |
|---|---|---|---|---|---|
| **Ideas** | • Has few, if any, original ideas.<br>• Lacks or has poorly developed characters, setting, plot, and conclusion.<br>• Has few, if any, details.<br>• Story line has little or no focus. | • Has some original ideas.<br>• Has minimally developed characters, setting, plot, and conclusion.<br>• Some details are present.<br>• Story focus strays. | • Has original ideas.<br>• Has fairly well-developed characters, setting, plot, and conclusion.<br>• Has some details that support the story.<br>• Generally maintains story focus. | • Has original ideas that tie-in with each other.<br>• Has fully-developed characters, setting, plot, and conclusion.<br>• Has carefully selected, interesting details that support the story.<br>• Maintains focus throughout. | |
| **Organization** | • Has little or no organization; lacks coherence.<br>• Lacks an introduction, body, and/or conclusion.<br>• Has no clear sequence of events or progression of plot.<br>• Is difficult to follow.<br>• Has no transitions between story parts. | • Some organization is present.<br>• Has an introduction, body, and conclusion, but may be unclear.<br>• Has plot progression, but some events are out of sequence.<br>• Is difficult to follow at times.<br>• Has few or ineffective transitions between story parts. | • Has logical organization.<br>• Has an introduction, body, and conclusion.<br>• Plot progresses sequentially and logically and is generally resolved in the conclusion.<br>• Is fairly easy to follow.<br>• Has transitions between some parts of the story. | • Has clear and logical organization.<br>• Has a complete introduction, body, and conclusion.<br>• Plot progresses and builds to a climax that is resolved in the conclusion.<br>• Is very easy to follow.<br>• Has smooth transitions between story parts. | |
| **Word Choice** | • Has few or no descriptions of characters and settings.<br>• Has a limited range of words that do not enhance the story.<br>• Words are not appropriate for purpose and audience.<br>• Words are used incorrectly.<br>• Word choice shows little thought and precision. | • Has some descriptions of characters and settings, but they are not very interesting.<br>• Uses passive verbs and few modifiers.<br>• Some words may not be appropriate for the audience and purpose.<br>• A few words are used incorrectly.<br>• Word choice includes some clichés and "tired" words. | • Has adequate descriptions of characters and setting.<br>• Uses some strong verbs and modifiers.<br>• Words are mostly appropriate for the audience and purpose.<br>• Words are used correctly but do not enhance the story.<br>• Words show thought and precision; clichés and "tired" words are avoided. | • Carefully chosen words make characters and setting interesting.<br>• Has many strong verbs and modifiers.<br>• Words are consistently appropriate for audience and purpose.<br>• Words are used correctly and enhance the story.<br>• Word choice is thoughtful and precise and includes some figurative language. | |

| | | | |
|---|---|---|---|
| **Sentence Fluency** | • Has no variation in sentence structures and lengths.<br>• Has no variation in sentence beginnings.<br>• Has no cadence or flow in paragraphs and sentences.<br>• Has forced, unnatural sounding dialogue. | • Has little variation in sentence structures and lengths.<br>• Has little variation in sentence beginnings.<br>• Paragraphs and sentences flow somewhat.<br>• Dialogue sometimes sounds unnatural. | • Has some variation in sentence structures and lengths.<br>• Has some variation in sentence beginnings.<br>• Paragraphs and sentences flow fairly naturally.<br>• Most dialogue sounds natural. | • Varied sentence structures and lengths contribute to the rhythm of the story.<br>• Varied sentence beginnings contribute to the flow of the story.<br>• Paragraphs and sentences flow naturally.<br>• Dialogue sounds natural. |
| **Voice** | • Writing is neither expressive nor engaging.<br>• Voice does not accurately reflect the character or narrator.<br>• Voice is not appropriate for the purpose, audience, topic, and/or genre. | • Writing has some expression.<br>• Voice somewhat reflects the character or narrator.<br>• Voice is generally appropriate for purpose, audience, topic, and/or genre. | • Writing is expressive and somewhat engaging.<br>• Voice reflects the character or narrator.<br>• Voice is appropriate for the purpose, audience, topic, and/or genre. | • Writing is very expressive and engaging.<br>• Voice accurately reflects the character or narrator of the story.<br>• Voice is appropriate for the purpose, audience, topic, and/or genre. |
| **Conventions** | • Has multiple errors in grammar, punctuation, and mechanics.<br>• Problems in the paragraph structure make the story hard to follow.<br>• Poor handwriting and/or presentation makes the story hard to read.<br>• Illustrations, if present, do not accurately portray the story. | • Has some errors in grammar, punctuation, and mechanics.<br>• Paragraph structure has some problems.<br>• Handwriting and/or presentation is fairly clear.<br>• Illustrations, if present, portray the story but do not enhance it. | • Has few errors in grammar, punctuation, and mechanics.<br>• Paragraph structure guides the reader through the story.<br>• Handwriting and/or presentation is clear.<br>• Illustrations, if present, accurately portray the story and enhance it somewhat. | • Has minimal errors in grammar, punctuation, and mechanics.<br>• Paragraph structure contributes to the organization and voice of the story.<br>• Handwriting and/or presentation of the piece is attractive and easy to read.<br>• Illustrations, if present, enhance the story significantly. |

**TOTAL**

# Part I: Learn the Parts of a Story

## Overview for the Teacher

Part I of this book presents a variety of activities to help students learn to identify and develop characters, setting, plot, and conclusions of stories.

 **Characters**
(pages 9–16)

These are the people, animals, or other creatures that the story is about. The main characters are those who have the most importance to the story. Often there are other characters who have smaller parts in the story. (See pages 9–16 for practice activities.)

As students determine the characters for their stories, they need to consider the point of view they will be using.

**First person**—The main character tells the story and uses *I*.

**Third person**—The story is told by a central observer and uses *she, he,* and *they* to recount the actions, thoughts, and feelings of the story's characters.

 **Setting**
(pages 17–24)

The setting includes the location and time in which the story takes place. These may change as the story progresses.

 **Plot**
(pages 25–31)

This is the plan of a story, including the problems, incidents, and/or actions that affect the characters and cause a reaction or a search for a solution or conclusion.

**Conclusion**
(pages 32–38)

This part of the story is the resolution of the problem or the final outcome of the story.

# Learn the Parts of a Story

## Characters

Select one or more of the following activities to introduce characters to your students:

**Identify the Characters** (page 10)
Choose a book that is familiar to the class. Ask, "Who are the main characters in this story?" Read aloud the parts that describe the characters.

List the characters on the board. Ask, "How does the author describe (name character)?" Write the descriptive words and phrases after the character's name.

Reproduce page 10 for each student. Using a book of their choice, have students list the main characters and write words and phrases used to describe them.

**Describe the Characters** (pages 11 and 12)
Have students select phrases that describe the characters shown in the illustration.

**Characters in a Story** (pages 13 and 14)
Have students write a description of one of the characters shown. Then have them read the description to a partner to see if the listener can select the correct character.

**Create a Character** (page 15)
Have students draw a character and then write a description of the character. Discuss words that might be used to describe the character's appearance and character traits (e.g., brave, lazy, daring).

Once the descriptions have been written, have students fold their papers to hide the drawing. They then give the descriptive paragraph to another student. That student draws a picture from the written description on a separate sheet of paper. Students then compare that picture with the original.

**My Story Plan: Characters** (page 16)
Discuss the types of stories students might write and what the plot might be. Explain to students that as they go through these lessons, they will be building a story; therefore, they should choose characters they want to write a complete story about. At this time, they should think about the story as a whole, but focus on the characters. Then have students use page 16 to plan a character list with descriptions for an original story. Provide students with a folder that they title "My Story Plan." Have them save page 16 in the folder. Later, they will add pages 24, 31, and 38.

Name: _____

# Identify the Characters

Title of Book: _____

Character: _____

Description: _____

_____

_____

Character: _____

Description: _____

_____

_____

Character: _____

Description: _____

_____

_____

Name: _____

# Describe the Characters

Underline the words and phrases that describe the girl.

Circle the words and phrases that describe the robot.

Make an **X** by the words and phrases that describe the dog.

You will not use all of the words or phrases.

| | | |
|---|---|---|
| responsible | brave | looks like a large silver man |
| falling apart | frightened | standing large and tall |
| needs help | small | big tail flying in the wind |
| frisky and noisy | friendly | dents and rusty places |
| reckless | strange | protects his owner |
| curious | strong | hates to be on a leash |
| curly ponytail | hair in a big bow | created to build doghouses |

Select one character. Using the descriptive words and phrases you marked, write a paragraph to introduce that character to your reader.

_____

_____

_____

_____

_____

Name: _____

# Describe the Characters

Underline the words and phrases that describe the zookeeper.

Circle the words and phrases that describe the monkey.

Make an **X** by the words and phrases that describe the elephant.

You will not use all of the words or phrases.

| | | |
|---|---|---|
| enormous | cares for animals | wearing work clothes |
| curious | chatters noisily | stands large and tall |
| strong | signs as he works | big ears flap back and forth |
| hardworking | little brown monkey | surprised |
| agile trunk | wet from head to toe | loves fruit |
| playful | wrinkled skin | whisks flies with its tail |
| ferocious | can swing on trees | standing on four big feet |

Select one character. Using the descriptive words and phrases you marked, write a paragraph to introduce that character to your reader.

_____

_____

_____

_____

_____

  How to Write a Story • EMC 794 • © Evan-Moor Corp.

Name: _____

# Characters in a Story

Choose one picture. Describe how the character looks and how you think he or she would act or behave. Make your description so clear that anyone will know which character you are writing about.

_____

_____

_____

_____

_____

_____

_____

_____

Name: _____

# Characters in a Story

Choose one picture. Describe how the character looks and how you think he or she would act or behave. Make your description so clear that anyone will know which character you are writing about.

_____

_____

_____

_____

_____

_____

_____

Name: _____

# Create a Character

Draw a character.

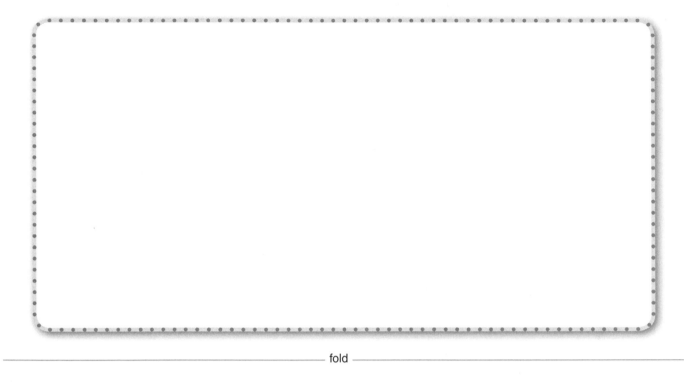

———————————————————————— fold ————————————————————————

Describe the character. Include appearance and character traits (how the character acts or behaves).

_____

_____

_____

_____

_____

_____

_____

Name: _____

# My Story Plan: Characters

Character: _____

Description: _____

_____

_____

Character: _____

Description: _____

_____

_____

Character: _____

Description: _____

_____

_____

# Learn the Parts of a Story

Select one or more of the following activities to introduce *setting* to your students:

### Identify the Setting (page 18)

Explain that the setting is both the location where the story takes place and the time in which it occurs. Then explain that time doesn't have to be exact (e.g., winter, during the Civil War, in the days of chivalry).

Refer to a familiar book or story. Read aloud parts that describe the setting. Ask, "Where does this story take place?" List the place on the board. Ask, "When does it take place?" List the time on the board. Have students give words or phrases that helped them identify the location and the time.

Explain that the setting may change as the story progresses. Use examples from literature to help students identify changing settings (either in location or time).

Reproduce page 18 for each student. Using a book of their choice, students list the setting and write words and phrases that describe the location and time.

### Describe the Setting (pages 19–22)

- For pages 19 and 20, have students select phrases that describe the setting shown in the illustration.

- For pages 21 and 22, have students write a description of one of the settings shown without naming it specifically. Then have them read the description to a partner to see if the listener can select the correct setting.

### Create a Setting (page 23)

Have students draw a setting and then write a description of the setting. Discuss words that might be used to describe the location and time.

Once the descriptions have been written, have students fold their papers to hide the drawing. They then give the descriptive paragraph to another student. That student draws a picture from the written description on a separate sheet of paper. Students then compare that picture with the original.

### My Story Plan: Setting (page 24)

Have students plan the setting, with descriptions, for the original story they began planning on page 16. Again, students should think about the story as a whole, but focus on the setting. Have them save this page in their "My Story Plan" folders.

Name: _____

# Identify the Setting

Title of Book: _____

Location: _____

Time: _____

List words and phrases describing the setting.

_____

_____

_____

_____

_____

Did the setting change as you read the story? How?

_____

_____

_____

_____

Name: _____

# Describe the Setting

Underline the phrases below that describe this setting.

| | | |
|---|---|---|
| long grass waving in the wind | cool breezes | dark shadows |
| elephant eating leaves | coiled snake | robins hunting worms |
| heat shimmering above the land | high noon | rolling sand dunes |
| elf owls hiding in holes | hot and dry | pools of cool water |
| grains of golden sand | giant cactus | hot winds blowing |
| icy snowflakes falling from the sky | night coming soon | strange night noises |

Using the underlined phrases, write a paragraph describing the setting to your readers.

_____

_____

_____

_____

_____

Name: _____

# Describe the Setting

Underline the phrases below that describe this setting.

| long kelp swaying in the water | rooster crowing | dark shadows |
| otter wrapped in kelp | crabs scuttling | sea stars on rocks |
| sunlight shimmering on the water | midnight | sharp cactus plants |
| octopus hiding under a rock | hot and dry | pools of cool water |
| grains of golden sand | school of fish | floating icebergs |
| tasty fruit growing on trees | rain falling | people talking |

Using the underlined phrases, write a paragraph describing the setting to your readers.

_____

_____

_____

_____

_____

How to Write a Story • EMC 794 • © Evan-Moor Corp.

Name: _____

# Describe the Setting

Choose one picture. Write a description of the setting. Make your description so clear that anyone will know which setting you are describing.

_____

_____

_____

_____

_____

_____

_____

_____

Name: _____

# Describe the Setting

Choose one picture. Write a description of the setting. Make your description so clear that anyone will know which setting you are describing.

_____

_____

_____

_____

_____

_____

_____

_____

Name: _____

# Create a Setting

Draw a setting.

———————————————————————— fold ————————————————————————

Describe the setting. Include location and time.

_____

_____

_____

_____

_____

_____

_____

Name: _____

# My Story Plan:
# Setting

Location: _____

Time: _____

Description: _____

_____

_____

_____

_____

_____

_____

_____

_____

_____

_____

# Learn the Parts of a Story

## Plot or Action

Select one or more of the following activities to introduce *plot* to your students:

### Identify the Plot (page 26)

Have students identify the plot elements in a favorite literature book. Select something that is short enough to read in one sitting. Remind students that the plot is the events or actions that affect the characters in the story. The plot includes the problems that have to be dealt with.

Read a portion of the story aloud to students. Ask, "What is the first important event that happens in the story?" List the event on the board. Continue reading sections of the story until all major plot elements are listed on the board.

Reproduce page 26 for each student. Using a book of their choice, students list the important actions and events that occur in the story.

### Describe the Plot (pages 27–30)

• For pages 27 and 28, have students identify possible story problems associated with the illustration. Then have them use the phrases to write a paragraph describing what is happening.

• For pages 29 and 30, have students describe two or three problems or events that fit one of the situations shown. Then have them read the description to a partner to see if the listener can select the correct illustration.

### My Story Plan: Plot (page 31)

Have students refer to their original character list (page 16) and setting descriptions (page 24). Using page 31, students write three problems or events the characters in that setting might experience. Students save this page in their "My Story Plan" folders.

Name: _____

# Identify the Plot

Title of Book: _____

List the important problems or events faced by the characters in this story.

_____

_____

_____

_____

_____

_____

_____

_____

_____

_____

_____

Name: _____

# Describe the Plot

Underline the phrases below that describe what is shown in this illustration.

| | | |
|---|---|---|
| hungry bear | storm coming | lost in the woods |
| broken leg | no way to escape | danger in the night |
| Dad out fishing | afraid to cry for help | caught up in a tree |
| hunter nearby | tree branch breaking | trapped in a cave |

Using the phrases you underlined, write a paragraph describing what is happening.

_____

_____

_____

_____

_____

Name: _____

# Describe the Plot

Underline the phrases that describe what is shown in this sequence of illustration.

| treasure hunter | no help in sight | dropping a fishing net |
| shark coming near | treasure chest in sand | colorful fish swimming by |
| diving into the water | fishermen in boat | gold coins spilled around |
| doesn't see danger | tentacles around chest | swimmer caught in kelp |

Using the phrases you underlined, write a paragraph describing what is happening.

_____

_____

_____

_____

_____

_____

# Describe the Plot

Choose one picture. Write a description of the situation that is illustrated. What else might happen? Make your description so clear that anyone will know which picture you are writing about.

_____

_____

_____

_____

_____

_____

_____

_____

Name: _____

# Describe the Plot

Choose one picture. Write a description of the situation that is illustrated. What else might happen? Make your description so clear that anyone will know which picture you are writing about.

_____

_____

_____

_____

_____

_____

_____

_____

  How to Write a Story • EMC 794 • © Evan-Moor Corp.

Name: _____

# My Story Plan: Plot

Think about what might happen to your characters if they were in the setting you described. Describe three problems or events that might occur in your story.

1. _____

_____

_____

_____

2. _____

_____

_____

_____

3. _____

_____

_____

_____

# Learn the Parts of a Story

## Conclusion

Select one or more of the following activities to introduce *conclusion* to your students:

### Identify the Conclusion (page 33)

Have students identify the conclusion in a favorite literature book. Select something that is short enough to read in one sitting. Remind students that the conclusion is the resolution of the problem or the final outcome of the story. It provides an ending that is clear and reasonable to the reader.

Review the problems or events in the story. Then read the concluding section to the students. Ask, "How does the author end the story? Does the ending solve the problems faced by the characters? Does the ending make sense?"

Reproduce page 33 for each student. Using a book of their choice, students describe the story's conclusion.

### Choose the Conclusion (pages 34 and 35)

Have students choose the best solution to a given problem. After explaining their choice, have students write an original conclusion.

### Write a Conclusion (pages 36 and 37)

Have students read a situation from a story and then write an appropriate conclusion. Share some of the conclusions with the class, comparing and contrasting the endings.

### My Story Plan: Conclusion (page 38)

Have students refer to their original plot form (page 31). Using page 38, students write a conclusion that resolves the problems or concludes the events set up on their plot action page.

### My Story

Have students put together the information on their "My Story Plan" sheets to write a complete story.

Name: _____

# Identify the Conclusion

Title of Book: _____

Describe the conclusion of this story.

_____

_____

_____

_____

_____

_____

_____

Do you think the author wrote a good conclusion for the story? Why or why not?

_____

_____

_____

_____

Name: _____

# Choose the Conclusion

**A boy's dog is stuck in a deep hole! What will happen?**

Here are some ways this problem might be solved. Choose the one you think is best.

☐ A friendly eagle was flying overhead. It flew down and picked up the dog. The eagle carried the dog to the boy.

☐ The boy heard the barking. He ran home to get his mom to help rescue the dog.

☐ The dog found a can of spinach in the hole. He ate the spinach, which gave him so much strength that he was able to jump out of the hole.

☐ A large gopher dug a tunnel from the hole to the surface. The dog crawled through the tunnel and ran home.

Explain why you picked this conclusion.

_____

_____

Now write a different conclusion to the same problem, using your imagination.

_____

_____

_____

Illustrate your conclusion.

# Choose the Conclusion

**An explorer is being held by a scary monster! What will happen?**

Here are some ways this problem might be solved. Choose the one you think is best.

☐ The explorer tickled the monster until it was laughing so hard that it couldn't hold on to her any longer.

☐ A tribe of friendly natives heard the explorer calling for help and rescued her.

☐ The explorer's dog nipped at the monster until the monster became so irritated that it let the explorer go.

☐ It turned out that the monster was trying to help by lifting the explorer out of the path of a herd of stampeding elephants.

Explain why you picked this conclusion.

_____

_____

Now write a different conclusion to the same problem, using your imagination.

_____

_____

_____

Illustrate your conclusion.

# Write a Conclusion

Read the story. Write an ending. Read your conclusion to someone to see if that person agrees that it is a reasonable ending.

> Jacob was excited. He and his mom had decided to hike to the top of Mt. Hook. It was hard work, but the view was awesome. Finally, they came to the bridge that hung between two cliffs.
>
> Jacob's mom pointed to the frayed rope. "This bridge looks different from the last time we were here. It could snap at any time!"
>
> Holding onto the railing, Jacob took a few steps on the bridge. "It feels fine," he said, taking a few more. Just as he got to the middle, he heard a rope snap. The bridge was coming apart!
>
> "Help!" Jacob yelled as he fell, clutching the rope.
>
> "Hang on, Jacob! Be strong!" his mom called. "I'll get help!" She quickly turned and ran. Jacob's arms were tired. It would take his mom a long time to reach the ranger station. "I can't give up," he thought.
>
> Before he knew it, a ranger appeared. "Jacob, we're going to pull you up!" the ranger yelled as he and Jacob's mom started lifting him to safety.

_____

_____

_____

_____

_____

_____

_____

Name: _____

# Write a Conclusion

Read the story. Write an ending. Read your conclusion to someone to see if that person agrees that it is a reasonable ending.

Everything had gone wrong for Harold this morning. He woke up late, he couldn't find his homework, and now he had missed the school bus. His mom had already left for work, so she couldn't take him.

"I know what to do," he thought. "I'll ride my bike. It's only a mile to school. I can still make it in time."

Harold went into the garage. "I don't believe this!" he groaned. His bike had a flat tire. Harold sat down and began to hit his head.

"Think, think," he whispered. "How am I going to get to school now?"

_____

_____

_____

_____

_____

_____

Name: _____

# My Story Plan: Conclusion

Think about the problems your characters have faced.
Write a conclusion that resolves these problems and ends your story.

_____

_____

_____

_____

_____

_____

_____

_____

_____

_____

_____

_____

# Part II: Write a Story Step by Step

## Prewrite

### Prepare a Writing Folder
- Staple the Story Checklist (page 42) to the outside of the folder.
- Staple a Story Plan Sheet (page 43 or 44) to the inside front cover.
- Writing forms (pages 45–49) should be placed inside the folder as they are completed.

### Brainstorm Topics
Have students brainstorm to create a list of possible topics and types of stories they could write.

You may choose to assign a specific genre and brainstorm appropriate topics within that genre. Students might write:

- realistic fiction
- historical fiction
- mystery
- adventure
- fantasy
- science fiction

### Use the Story Plan Sheets
Students begin the writing process by thinking about the story as a whole so they have a definite direction as they write.

Students may use either of the Story Plan Sheets on pages 43 and 44 to plan the stories.

Beginning or reluctant writers may need individual help in getting their stories started. Less experienced writers might also benefit from drawing their characters and setting.

## Write a Rough Draft

If this is the first time your students have used planning forms, do each page as a guided lesson. As students gain experience, you may want to distribute all of the planning forms (page 43 or 44 and pages 45–49) at the same time so students can work on stories at their own pace.

### Draft a Story (pages 45–49)

Students use the information from their Story Plan Sheets to fill in the rough draft pages. Provide extra paper for students who need more writing space.

1. **Beginning the Story**—Who, Where, and When?

   Using page 45, students write the introduction to their story. The main characters are introduced and the setting is established. Writers should gain the reader's interest by using colorful and exciting language.

2. **Plot Action**—What Happened and Why?

   A story may have fewer than three points of plot action. However, three points create a well-rounded, interesting story. More than three are difficult for young authors to deal with.

   *Plot Action 1*

   Using page 46, students begin writing the first action section of their plot by describing WHO did WHAT, WHEN, and WHY.

   *Plot Action 2*

   Using page 47, students write the middle of the story. Remind them that they are about halfway through the story and that the action should be continuing to build.

   *Plot Action 3*

   Using page 48, students write the climax of the story. This should be the most exciting and suspenseful point in the story.

3. **Conclusion**

   Using page 49, students write a conclusion to their stories. The story ending should resolve the problems and be consistent with the actions in the story.

## Revise the Story

### 1. Read Aloud

Encourage the author to read the story aloud to a partner and/or have a partner read the story aloud as the author listens. Have partners discuss the following questions:

> Does the story sound the way I want it to? Is more description or detail needed?
>
> Does the story make sense? Are events in the correct order?
>
> Does the ending fit the rest of the story?

### 2. Make Revisions

Students use the feedback from the read aloud to make revisions and improve their stories. When satisfied that the ideas are more interesting, that the story is in order, that the wording is clear, and that the ending is the best possible choice, students may move on to the next step.

## Edit the Story

Have students reread their stories, paying special attention to accuracy in the conventions of written language. They should check the story for correct grammar, capitalization, punctuation, and spelling, making corrections where needed.

Then have students work with a partner to proofread their stories and make corrections.

## Finalize the Title

Have students evaluate the title they chose before beginning to write the story. Does it really describe what the story is about? If not, select a few words that describe the characters and the main theme of the story. Have students use these words to develop at least three possible story titles. Have the author discuss these titles with classmates, asking what they think the story is about. Then the author selects the best of the three as the title of the story.

## Write the Final Copy

Occasionally, you may wish to have your students produce a final copy of a story. Have students make a clean copy of their story and, if desired, illustrate it.

Name: _____

# Story Checklist

☐ **Spend time thinking about the:**

    _____ type of story (genre)

    _____ main idea for plot

    _____ title

☐ **Complete Story Plan Sheet**

☐ **Write Rough Draft**

☐ **Revise Story—Content**

    _____ read aloud

    _____ made revisions

☐ **Edit Story—Mechanics**

    _____ spelling

    _____ punctuation and capitalization

    _____ grammar

☐ **Write Final Copy**

☐ **Illustrate Story**

☐ **Make a Cover**

☐ **Share the Story with Others**

Name: _____

# Story Plan Sheet

Story Title: _____

**Character(s)**—Who

_____

_____

_____

_____

**Setting**—Where and When

_____

_____

_____

_____

**Plot**—What Happened and Why

1. _____

_____

2. _____

_____

3. _____

_____

**Conclusion**—The End

_____

_____

_____

Name: _____

# Story Plan Sheet

Story Title: _____

List and describe the main **characters**.

_____

_____

_____

_____

_____

Describe the main **setting** of your story.

_____

_____

Think about the **plot**. What will happen in your story?

_____

_____

_____

Describe the **conclusion** of your story.

_____

_____

_____

Name: _____

# Beginning the Story

## Who, Where, and When

Write a paragraph to introduce your story. This is where you want to catch the reader's interest, so think of an exciting, funny, or mysterious way to start the story. Include a description of the main character or characters. Describe where and when the story takes place. Use more paper if you need to.

_____

_____

_____

_____

_____

_____

_____

_____

_____

_____

Name: _____

# Plot Action 1

Tell **WHO** did **WHAT**, **WHEN**, and **WHY**.

This is the first **ACTION**.

This is the place to get the story moving.

_____

_____

_____

_____

_____

_____

_____

_____

_____

_____

_____

_____

_____

Name: _____

# Plot Action 2

This is the second **ACTION**.

Now your character is halfway through the story.

This is the place to help readers understand the problems your character is facing.

_____

_____

_____

_____

_____

_____

_____

_____

_____

_____

_____

_____

# Plot Action 3

This is the **CLIMAX** of your story.

It should be the most exciting part.

_____

_____

_____

_____

_____

_____

_____

_____

_____

_____

_____

_____

# Conclusion

This is the **ENDING**.

It must relate to the **ACTION** in the story.

This is where the problems are resolved and the story is brought to a satisfactory end.

_____

_____

_____

_____

_____

_____

_____

_____

_____

_____

# Part III: Additional Story-Planning Forms

The following pages contain several types of graphic organizers to use for planning stories. They provide students with alternatives for writing different types of stories. Be sure to model each new process when you introduce it to your students. You may need to guide students through the steps several times before they are comfortable with the process.

## Outline (page 51)

Students follow a simple outline format to organize a story.

## 5 Ws and an H (page 52)

Students answer the questions Who? Did What? Where? When? How? and Why? to create a story outline.

## A Story Web (page 53)

Students organize the parts of the story on a web, including areas for character(s), setting, plot actions, and a story conclusion.

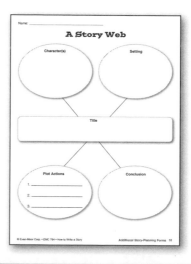

Name: _____

# Story Outline

_____
(working title)

## I. Character(s)

A. _____

B. _____

C. _____

## II. Setting

A. Location _____

B. Time _____

## III. Plot Actions

A. _____

B. _____

C. _____

## IV. Conclusion

_____

_____

_____

Name: _____

# 5 Ws and an H

**Who?** _____

_____

_____

**Did What?** _____

_____

_____

**Where?** _____

_____

_____

**When?** _____

_____

_____

**How?** _____

_____

_____

**Why?** _____

_____

_____

Name: _____

# A Story Web

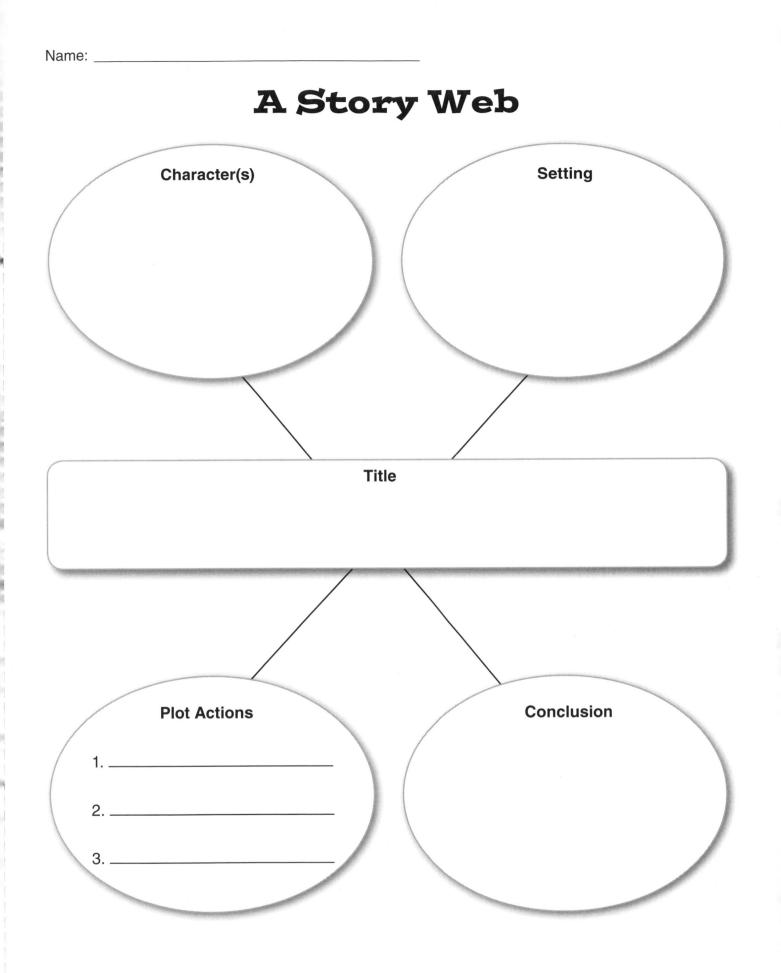

**Character(s)**

**Setting**

**Title**

**Plot Actions**

1. _____

2. _____

3. _____

**Conclusion**

# Part IV: Write in Different Genres

Once students have mastered the steps for writing a story, challenge them to write in specific fiction genres. As with all writing experiences, it is important to read and analyze samples of each genre in order to understand its specific elements. These authors often write in specific genres for ages 9–12:

### Realistic Fiction
(pages 55 and 56)

Beverly Cleary
Cynthia DeFelice
Jack Gantos
Jessie Haas
E.L. Konigsburg
Lois Lowry
Katherine Paterson
Richard Peck
Pamela Muñoz Ryan
Cynthia Rylant
Louis Sachar
Jerry Spinelli
Suzanne Fisher Staples

### Historical Fiction
(pages 57 and 58)

Avi
Christopher Paul Curtis
Karen Cushman
Paula Fox
Patricia Reilly Giff
Virginia Hamilton
Karen Hesse
Irene Hunt
Louise Moeri
Walter Dean Myers
Ann Rinaldi
Mildred D. Taylor

### Mystery
(pages 59 and 60)

Linda Bailey
Mary Downing Hahn
Tami Hoag
James Howe
Dave Keane
Jean Lowery Nixon
Elvira Woodruff
Betty Ren Wright

### Adventure
(pages 61 and 62)

Natalie Babbitt
Dave Barry and
Ridley Pearson
Georgia Byng
Sharon Creech
Jean Craighead George
Will Hobbs
Ben Mikaelsen
Phyllis Reynolds Naylor
Gary Paulsen

### Fantasy
(pages 63 and 64)

Bruce Coville
Tony DiTerlizzi and
Holly Black
Cornelia Funke
Brian Jacques
Ursula K. Le Guin
Gail Carson Levine
Robin McKinley
Tamora Pierce
Philip Pullman
Angie Sage
Jon Scieszka
Laurence Yep
Jane Yolen

### Science Fiction
(pages 65 and 66)

K.A. Applegate
Betsy Byars
Orson Scott Card
Eoin Colfer
Bruce Coville
Nancy Farmer
Madeleine L'Engle
Anne McCaffrey

# Write in Different Genres

*Realistic fiction is a story based on events that could really happen. The characters, setting, and details seem real. These are stories that help us learn more about ourselves and other people.*

- Read examples of realistic fiction to the class. Analyze each story, identifying characters (protagonist, antagonist, and secondary characters), plot actions leading up to the climax, and the resolution or conclusion that ends the story. Determine the point of view from which the story is told (first person or third person). Determine the tone in which the story is written (humorous, sad, serious, or a combination of these).

- Introduce or review terms that might be confusing to students:

   **protagonist**—the central character of the story

   **antagonist**—the character that is creating the conflict

   **secondary characters**—the extra characters that help move the story along

   **first person point of view**—the story is written as though it is being told by the main character; *I* is used throughout the story

   **third person point of view**—the story is written from a storyteller's perspective

   **tone**—the writer's attitude toward the subject

   **conflict**—the plot actions or problems that the characters encounter

   **climax**—the most exciting event, usually built up from the preceding conflicts

   **resolution/conclusion**—resolution of the conflicts and the ending of the story

- Provide the Realistic Fiction question sheet (page 56) and story planning forms (pages 42–49) or graphic organizers (pages 51–53) to assist students in planning their stories.

# Realistic Fiction

Realistic fiction is a story based on events that could really happen. The characters, setting, and details seem real.

1. Who are the **characters** going to be? Who is the main character? What other characters will there be?

   a. What are the characters' names?

   b. What do they look like?

   c. What kind of personality does each character have?

2. What is the **setting** going to be?

   a. What will the location be like?

   b. When does the story take place?

   c. Will the setting change as the story progresses?

3. What **point of view** will you use—first person or third person?

4. Think about the story **events**. As you plan the events, think about how the main characters will react to them.

   a. What events or problems will occur in the story? Try to have at least three.

   b. What will the climax be? Remember, it should be the most exciting event.

   c. How will the main character resolve the conflict?

5. Use a planning form to outline the basic story information.

   a. The **beginning** should establish the characters and setting.

   b. The **middle** should describe the story events, including the climax.

   c. Plan how the story will **end**.

# Write in Different Genres

**Write Historical Fiction**

*Historical fiction is a kind of realistic fiction. It is an invented story based on a historical event. The time and place of the setting are real and are portrayed authentically. Some characters may also be historical figures. Historical fiction may portray real people in invented situations or invented people in historical settings.*

- Read examples of historical fiction to the class. Analyze each story, identifying the historical parts. When and where does the story take place? Which characters are historical figures and which are invented? What events in the story are historical and which are the author's inventions?

  Once you have established the historical aspects, identify the other story elements such as plot events leading up to the climax and the resolution or conclusion that ends the story, and determine the point of view from which the story is told (first person or third person). As with other realistic fiction, the story may be written in various tones—humorous, sad, serious, or a combination of these.

- Introduce or review terms that might be confusing to students. (See the list on page 55.)

  Because there must be historical truth in these stories, you may wish to restrict students to what has been studied in social studies that year. Brainstorm with students to create charts that list events, characters, and settings. Display these charts as students plan their stories.

- Review the points students need to consider in planning their stories, and provide support as they develop their story outlines.

- Provide the Historical Fiction question sheet (page 58) and story planning forms (pages 42–49) or graphic organizers (pages 51–53) to assist students in planning their stories.

# Historical Fiction

Historical fiction is a kind of realistic fiction. It is a story based on a person or an event from history. The time and place of the setting are real.

1. Who are the **characters** going to be? Are they historical characters or will you invent them? Who is the main character? What other characters will there be?

    a. What are the characters' names?

    b. What do they look like?

    c. What kind of personality does each character have?

2. What is the **setting** going to be? Remember, in historical fiction the setting must be real.

    a. What is the location?

    b. When does the story take place?

    c. Will the setting change as the story progresses?

3. What **point of view** will you use—first person or third person?

4. Think about the story **events**. Are the events historical or will you invent them? As you plan the events, think about how the main characters will react to them.

    a. What events or problems will occur in the story? Try to have at least three.

    b. What will the climax be? Remember, it should be the most exciting event.

    c. How will the main character resolve the conflict?

5. Use a planning form to outline the basic story information.

    a. The **beginning** should establish the characters and setting.

    b. The **middle** should describe the story events, including the climax.

    c. Plan how the story will **end**.

# Write in Different Genres

*A mystery story is filled with suspense and contains a problem or a crime to solve. The plot contains the clues that lead the main character to the solution. A mystery usually contains the person doing the detective work, a victim, a wrongdoer, and other suspects that are found out to be innocent. Unexpected and imaginative events and settings add to the suspense in a mystery story.*

- Read examples of mystery stories to the class. Analyze each story, identifying the mystery or crime. Look for the clues that are provided to help solve the mystery. Are "red herrings" (false clues) included to confuse the reader? Explain that in a good mystery, the reader should have enough clues to solve the mystery if he or she reads the story carefully.

- Help students understand that a mystery story has certain elements that should be included in their own stories. The characters in a mystery each have a specific part to play. The main character has to look for clues and solve the problem. There is often a "wrongdoer" who is the perpetrator of the crime or creator of the story conflict. The secondary characters serve as suspects that are proved innocent as the story progresses.

  The plot of a mystery usually involves a crime or a mysterious secret. Clues can be objects such as fingerprints, bits of clothing, footprints, notes, or hints given by the speech or actions of characters in the story.

  Mystery stories are frequently written in the first person, but may also be written in the third person.

- Introduce or review terms that might be confusing to students. (See the list on page 55.)

- Review the points students need to consider in planning their stories. Remind them that the most important questions to think about as they write a mystery are "Who did it?" "What happened?" and "Why?"

- Provide the Mystery Story question sheet (page 60) and story planning forms (pages 42–49) or graphic organizers (pages 51–53) to assist students in planning their stories.

# Mystery Story

A mystery story contains a problem or a crime to solve and the clues that lead the main character to the solution. Unexpected events and innocent suspects add to the suspense.

1. What kind of mystery is it going to be? Is there a crime? Is there a secret to find out about? If there is a crime, think about who did it and why that person did it.

2. Who are the **characters** going to be? Most mysteries contain a detective, a victim, a wrongdoer, and one or more innocent suspects. Think about which characters will be in your story.

    a. What are the characters' names?

    b. What do they look like?

    c. What kind of personality does each character have?

    d. What is the wrongdoer's motive for committing the crime?

3. What is the **setting** going to be?

    a. What is the location?

    b. When does the story take place?

    c. Will the setting change as the story progresses?

4. What **point of view** will you use—first person or third person?

5. Think about the story **events**.

    a. What crime is going to occur, or what secret is going to be discovered?

    b. What clues will help solve the mystery?

    c. Who will be suspected of the crime but be proved innocent?

    d. What clue will finally allow the main character to solve the crime?

6. Use a planning form to outline the basic story information.

    a. The **beginning** should establish the mystery, the characters, and the setting.

    b. The **middle** should describe the events of the crime or secret and reveal the clues, with the most important clue coming at the story climax.

    c. Plan how the story will **end**. This is where the wrongdoer is identified or the mystery is solved.

# Write in Different Genres

## Write an Adventure Story

*An adventure story is one in which the main character or characters must overcome great obstacles. There is usually an important task to be completed or a goal to be reached. This type of story is filled with fast-moving action, often involving an exciting journey to interesting places. The setting changes frequently as the characters move from one event to the next.*

- Read examples of adventure stories to the class. Analyze each story, identifying the main theme. Is there a hidden treasure? Is the main character exploring a new land? Is there some secret to be discovered? Identify the characters (the main character is often called the hero or heroine in an adventure story), the plot events leading up to the climax, and the resolution or conclusion that ends the story. If the story is about hidden treasure or a secret, what clues are provided that help the main character find the treasure or unravel the secret?

- Determine the point of view from which the story is told (first person or third person) and the style being used. Help students understand that adventure stories can be humorous, serious, or a combination of the two, as long as the story is fast moving. In fact, action is one of the most important elements of a good adventure story.

- Introduce or review terms that might be confusing to students. (See the list on page 55.)

- Provide the Adventure Story question sheet (page 62) and story planning forms (pages 42–49) or graphic organizers (pages 51–53) to assist students in planning their stories.

# Adventure Story

In an adventure story, the main character or characters must overcome great obstacles. There is an important task to be completed or a goal to be reached. The story is filled with fast-moving action. There may be an exciting journey to interesting places.

1. What kind of adventure is it going to be? Is there a hidden treasure? Is there a secret to reveal? Will the main character discover a new and mysterious land?

2. Who are the **characters** going to be? Most adventure stories contain a hero and/or heroine, someone who tries to stop the main character, and other less important characters.

   a. What are the characters' names?

   b. What do they look like?

   c. What kind of personality does each character have?

3. What is the **setting** going to be?

   a. What is the main location?

   b. When does the story take place?

   c. How will the settings change as the story progresses?

4. What **point of view** will you use—first person or third person?

5. Think about the story **events**. As you plan, think about how the characters will react to them.

   a. What is the purpose of the story? Is the main character searching for hidden treasure? Trying to reveal a secret? Discovering an unexplored land?

   b. If there is hidden treasure or a secret, what clues will you provide?

   c. What events or problems will occur in the story? Try to have at least three.

   d. What will the climax be? Remember that it should be the most exciting event.

   e. How will you end the story?

6. Use a planning form to outline the basic story information.

   a. The **beginning** should establish the basis for the adventure and introduce the main character.

   b. The **middle** should describe the story events, with the most important clue coming at the story climax.

   c. Plan how the story will **end**.

# Write in Different Genres

*Make-believe and talking animals and other imaginary characters are important parts of a fantasy story. Some or all of the story elements (characters, setting, problems, events, and solution) are imaginary and would be impossible in the real world.*

- Read examples of fantasy stories to the class. Analyze each story, identifying the characters, the plot events leading up to the climax, and the resolution or conclusion that ends the story. Identify the parts of the story that are from the author's imagination. Was the story set in the real world with imaginary characters? Was it set in an imaginary world with real characters? What happens in the story that would be impossible in real life?

- Explain to students that the characters in fantasy stories are almost always either very good or very bad. Also, animals and inanimate objects sometimes act in human ways by talking, walking, etc. A fantasy story ends with some resolution to a conflict, usually with good overcoming evil.

- Introduce or review terms that might be confusing to students. (See the list on page 55).

- Provide the Fantasy Story question sheet (page 64) and story planning forms (pages 42–49) or graphic organizers (pages 51–53) to assist students in planning their stories.

# Fantasy Story

Make-believe and talking animals and other imaginary characters are important parts of a fantasy story. Characters are often very good or very bad. Good usually wins over evil. Some or all of the story comes from the writer's imagination and would be impossible in the real world.

1. Where is your story going to begin?

2. What is the **setting** going to be?

   a. the real world

   b. an imaginary world

3. Who are the **characters** going to be? Decide if you are going to have animals or objects that act like people in your story.

   a. What are the characters' names?

   b. What do they look like?

   c. What kind of personality does each character have?

4. What **point of view** will you use—first person or third person?

5. Think about the story **events**. As you plan, think about how the characters will react to them.

   a. What happens to the main character?

   b. What events or problems will occur in the story? Try to have at least three.

   c. What will the climax be? Remember that it should be the most exciting event.

   d. How will you end the story?

6. Use a planning form to outline the basic story information.

   a. The **beginning** should introduce the main character, describe the world in which the story begins, and introduce the character's problem.

   b. The **middle** should describe the story events. The most important event comes at the story climax.

   c. Plan how the story will **end**. How will the main character's problem be resolved?

# Write in Different Genres

*Science fiction is a special kind of fantasy story. The story elements that are unreal are based on scientific possibilities. The story is usually set in the future. Technology, space travel, and aliens are often a part of science fiction stories. The story might involve robots, unusual computers, space travel, imaginative inventions, other dimensions, or future events.*

• Read examples of science fiction to the class. Analyze each story, identifying the characters, the plot events leading up to the climax, and the resolution or conclusion that ends the story. Science fiction stories are usually set in the future. Identify the parts of the story describing the setting. How can we tell when this story takes place? What happens in the story that is based on science? What parts of the story are imaginary? (These could be characters, animals, vehicles, tools, locations, etc.) What happens in the story that would be impossible in our lives today?

• Explain to students that science fiction is a form of fantasy. It can also contain elements of a good adventure. The main difference is that what happens must be based on real science. In science fiction, the setting can be on Earth at a future time, on another planet, in space aboard a spaceship, or on a space station. The characters can be human, alien, or robots, but the elements of a good story still count. The characters must be interesting, the plot must contain events that lead to an exciting climax, and the conclusion must make sense.

• Introduce or review terms that might be confusing to students. (See the list on page 55.) Review the points students need to consider in planning their stories, and provide support as they develop their story outlines.

• Provide the Science Fiction question sheet (page 66) and story planning forms (pages 42–49) or graphic organizers (pages 51–53) to assist students in planning their stories.

# Science Fiction

Science fiction is a kind of fantasy. The story is usually set in the future. Technology, space travel, and aliens are often a part of science fiction stories. The story might be about robots, unusual computers, space travel, unusual inventions, other dimensions, or future events.

1. Where is your story going to begin—on Earth in the future, on another planet, aboard a spaceship, or on a space station?

2. What is the **setting** going to be?

3. Who are the **characters** going to be? Characters can be humans, aliens, or unusual characters such as robots or computers.

   a. What are the characters' names?

   b. What do they look like?

   c. What kind of personality does each character have?

4. What **point of view** will you use—first person or third person?

5. Think about the story **events**. As you plan, think about how the characters will react to them. Remember, whatever equipment or means of transportation that is used in the story must have some basis in real science.

   a. What events or problems will occur in the story? Try to have at least three.

   b. What will the climax be? Remember that it should be the most exciting event.

   c. How will you end the story?

6. Use a planning form to outline the basic story information.

   a. The **beginning** should introduce the main character, describe the world in which the action will occur, and introduce the character's problem.

   b. The **middle** should describe the story events. This is where events build up to the story climax.

   c. Plan how the story will **end**.

# Part V: Presentation

Not all story-writing experiences will be taken beyond the editing step. The following steps are for those stories that are to be published in a final form.

## Make a Final Copy

Students will recopy their edited stories to make a clear, easy-to-read copy. This may be done by hand or on a computer.

### Write by Hand

Provide an ample supply of writing materials such as pens, pencils, colored pencils, and interesting types of paper, as well as the templates on pages 68–71. The templates provide a means to arrange the story in various interesting ways on the pages. Open spaces are left for illustrations. Extend the life of the templates by laminating them.

1. Select one or more template forms to use.

2. Fasten a blank sheet of paper over the form using a paper clip.

3. Write the story on the lines.

4. Remove the paper clip.

5. Create illustrations inside the blank spaces.

### Write on a Computer

1. Type the story.

2. Edit and spell check.

3. Format the text.
   a. select a font (one the author and audience can easily read)
   b. select a type size

4. Illustrate the story using the computer drawing tools or found images. Insert the pictures in the completed text document.

5. Print out the story.

## Illustrate the Story

Some students will want to have whole-page illustrations as a part of their stories. Provide a variety of types of paper and art materials to use in illustrating stories.

## Publish the Story

Pages 72–74 provide forms for students to create title, dedication, and "About the Author" pages.

## Bind the Story

Page 75 provides ideas on how to put student books together.

# Presentation

## Special Pages

Reproduce the forms on pages 73 and 74 to add the following types of pages to a book. Have students cut out the special page frames and glue them onto pages in their books.

### Title Page

Include the title, author, illustrator, room number, school, and date. If your class has given its in-class publishing center a special name, this may be used instead of a room number.

### Dedication Page

Have the authors dedicate their stories to someone special or to someone who was especially helpful in writing them.

### About the Author

Have the authors describe themselves, including likes, dislikes, and special interests. Have them explain why they chose the subjects of their stories. Invite them to include a school photograph if one is available, or have the author draw a self-portrait to include in this section.

page 73

page 74

**Title**

**Author**

**Illustrator**

**Room Number/School**

**Date**

Note: Cut these forms apart. Glue each section onto a separate page.

# About the Author

_____

_____

_____

_____

_____

_____

_____

_____

_____

# Dedication

_____

_____

_____

_____

_____

_____

_____

_____

# Presentation

Bookbinding can be as simple as stapling a story between two sheets of construction paper. However, if you and your students have taken the time to carefully write a story, you may want to make a special binding and cover for the books.

## Three Quick and Easy Covers

Staple the cover to the story pages. Cover the staples with a strip of tape.

Punch holes through the cover and story pages. Put the book together with metal rings.

Punch holes through the cover and story pages. Tie the book together with shoelaces, yarn, or sturdy string.

## Hinged Covers

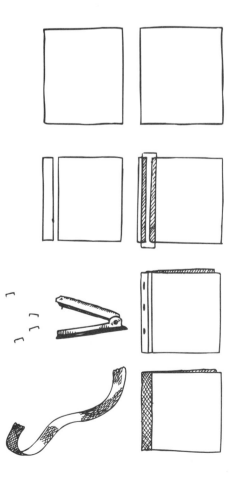

1. Cut two pieces of poster board, cardboard, etc., slightly larger than the story pages.

2. Cut a ½" (1.25 cm) strip from the left-hand side of the front cover. Tape the strips together on the inside. Leave a small space open between the two strips.

3. Staple the cover and story pages together. Cover the front hinge and the front and back staples with a 1½" (4 cm) piece of cloth book tape.

# Part VI: Writing and Publishing Centers

Set up one or both of the following centers. The Writing Center contains materials and story prompts to encourage independent story writing. The Publishing Center provides the materials needed to turn a story into a book.

## Setting up a Writing Center

### Equipment and Supplies

- writing paper of different sizes and types
- a bookcase or shelf to hold materials
- a table or other work area in front of a bulletin board
- a computer and printer
- writing implements, such as pencils and pens

### Planning Aids

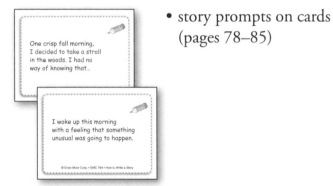

- graphic organizers to use in planning stories (pages 51–53)

- story prompts on cards (pages 78–85)

- charts containing character, setting, and plot lists (pages 86–89)

- charts containing steps for writing stories in different genres (pages 90–95)

## Setting up a Publishing Center

Use any or all of the following items:

- a table or other work area in front of a bulletin board

- a bookcase or shelf to hold materials

- materials for illustrating books:

| | |
|---|---|
| crayons | colored paper |
| colored pencils | magazines |
| markers | scissors |
| paint | glue |
| paintbrushes | |

- templates (pages 68–71) for students to use in writing and illustrating

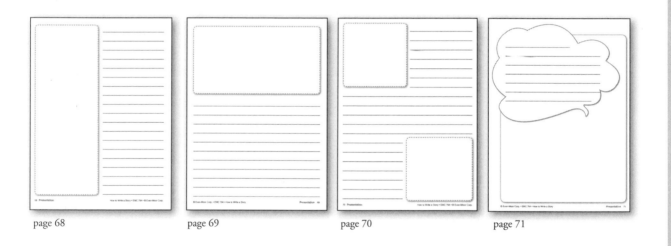

page 68        page 69        page 70        page 71

- materials for making covers:

| | | |
|---|---|---|
| mat board | wrapping paper | cloth tape |
| poster board | self-adhesive paper | duct tape |
| cardboard | brown paper grocery bags | needle and thread |
| construction paper | cloth | shoelaces |
| newspaper | cellophane tape | yarn |
| wallpaper | masking tape | string |

- a spiral-binding machine to attach covers

One crisp fall morning, I decided to take a stroll in the woods. I had no way of knowing that...

© Evan-Moor Corp. • EMC 794 • How to Write a Story

I woke up this morning with a feeling that something unusual was going to happen.

© Evan-Moor Corp. • EMC 794 • How to Write a Story

(Name) was horrified to discover that he/she was slowly shrinking.

© Evan-Moor Corp. • EMC 794 • How to Write a Story

The door to our classroom slowly opened and in walked...

© Evan-Moor Corp. • EMC 794 • How to Write a Story

Bubbles was an old dog. She had always been the only pet in the family. Now her owner had brought home two little kittens...

Jerome was looking for his lost soccer ball. Instead, he found...

During a terrible storm, our boat crashed onto an undiscovered island. I wonder what we'll find when we start to explore it?

Krystal and her dad went fishing at the lake. When she pulled in her hook and line, she saw...

A mother deer hid her newborn fawn under a bush while she searched for food. While she was gone...

"My bike has a flat tire. What do I do now?" Lester didn't know that help was already coming his way.

Pete needed money to buy a birthday gift. He had to think of a way to earn some money. "I've got an idea!" he shouted.

After a long winter's rest, the big brown bear woke up in his cave. The bear poked his head out of the cave and saw...

My best friend (name) was jumping up and down with excitement. "I think I've discovered a time machine!" (name) shouted.

My birthday celebration was not what I expected. Everything was very strange.

Abigail looked out her bedroom window to see what was making so much noise. She saw...

Write a story about the adventure you would have if you traded places with (name).

Write a fantasy story about dragons, a timid knight, and a brave princess.

The blizzard had been raging for a week. The TV didn't work, and I was sick of all my toys. Suddenly, I had a great idea. I would...

(Name) and (name) were putting the finishing touches on their magnificent snowperson, when they heard a strange voice.

A spacecraft from a distant galaxy has just landed on Earth. The voyagers are curious about...

Write a story about what would happen if you woke up one morning and could fly.

Jerome had promised his grandmother that he would help dig up ground for a vegetable garden. Suddenly, his shovel hit something hard under the ground...

Write a mysterious story that will give your reader the shivers.

While Angela was looking in the lost and found for her missing lunchbox, she discovered...

Old sayings can be wrong. This year's April showers didn't bring May flowers. Instead, they brought...

Imagine that you just bought a pair of sunglasses. When you look through them, you discover that you can see into the future.

It had been a pretty dull summer. Then (name) moved in next door.

Let me tell you about the crazy sleepover I went to this weekend.

You have been blamed for a crime you did not commit. Now you must prove your innocence.

Choose four people from history. Write a story about what would happen if they were lost in a forest together.

Emily never thought she was anyone special. Then one day, a strange visitor showed up at her door...

Ever since Tyler's mom was elected president, his life was one adventure after another.

# Pick a Character

worn-out shoe

new kid in school

pesky little kitten

substitute teacher

Uncle Moe and Aunt Tillie

polar bear with a problem

cranky baby sitter

tired, dirty stray dog

alien from outer space

mischievous monkey

gigantic octopus

newly discovered animal

talking garbage can

eager salesperson

daring explorer

timid dragon

brave princess

noisy children

lazy farmer

three-legged dog

circus acrobat

grumpy teacher

astronaut

famous singer

grandparents

best friends

soccer team

inventor

# Pick a Setting
## Location

inside my pocket

at the zoo

on a faraway planet

in the backyard

in a rainforest

at the park

outside my door

up in a tree

in a secret hiding place

near the school

along the path

under my bed

on a float in a parade

downtown

under the sea

at Grandmother's

on the beach

in the garden

through dark woods

on the moon

up on the roof

inside a cave

in Paris, France

next door

at an amusement park

at a swimming pool

in a dark garage

under a pile of dirt

# Pick a Setting
## Time

| | |
|---|---|
| noon | in the fourth grade |
| midnight | during the movie |
| on my birthday | after the soccer game |
| last year | when I was a baby |
| before school | one stormy night |
| just now | during a hurricane |
| before you came | during a snowstorm |
| Independence Day | an hour ago |
| yesterday | when the plane landed |
| this morning | long, long ago |
| soon | once upon a time |
| in 2050 | as the sun set |
| this morning | recently |
| about six o'clock | after school |

   How to Write a Story • EMC 794 • © Evan-Moor Corp.

# Pick a Plot

| | |
|---|---|
| a terrible accident | strange footprints |
| a stolen bike | traveling into the past |
| winning a contest | pizza has been outlawed |
| what a big mess | rescuing a cat in a tree |
| camping by a river | waking up with blue hair |
| caught in a blizzard | stranded on an island |
| a lost pet | suddenly being invisible |
| seeing a falling star | a fight with a friend |
| meeting a wild bear | being a new kid in school |
| going to the circus | finding a bag of money |
| buying new shoes | in charge of school |
| meeting (name) | finding a treasure map |
| going into outer space | discovering a planet |
| working in a (name a place) | carried off by an eagle |

# Write Realistic Fiction

1. Name and describe story characters.

2. Describe the time and location of the setting.

3. Select a point of view to use—first person or third person.

4. Plan story events.
   a. What will happen?
   b. What will the climax be?
   c. How will the story end?

5. Outline the basic information.
   a. Beginning—Establish the characters and setting.
   b. Middle—Describe events, including the climax.
   c. End—Plan how the story will end.

6. Write your story.

# Write Historical Fiction

1.  Name and describe story characters.
    Are they historical or invented?

2.  Describe the time and location of the setting.
    Remember that in historical fiction, the setting must
    be real.

3.  Select a point of view to use—first person or third person.

4.  Plan story events.
    Are events historical or invented?
    a. What will happen?
    b. What will the climax be?
    c. How will the story end?

5.  Outline the basic information.
    a. Beginning—Establish the characters and setting.
    b. Middle—Describe events, including the climax.
    c. End—Plan how the story will end.

6.  Write your story.

# Write a Mystery Story

1. What kind of mystery is it going to be—crime, puzzle, or secret?

2. Name and describe story characters.
   Most mysteries have a detective, a victim, a wrongdoer, and innocent suspects.

3. Describe the time and location of the setting.

4. Select a point of view to use—first person or third person.

5. Plan story events.
   Don't forget to include clues that help solve the mystery. You may want to include a suspect that is proved innocent.
   - a. What will happen?
   - b. What will the climax be?
   - c. How will the story end?

6. Outline the basic information.
   - a. Beginning—Establish the characters and setting.
   - b. Middle—Describe events, including the climax.
   - c. End—Plan how the story will end.

7. Write your story.

# Write an Adventure Story

1. What kind of adventure is it going to be—hidden treasure, a secret to reveal, or discovering a new land?

2. Name and describe story characters.

3. Describe the time and location of the setting. Remember, the setting often changes several times in an adventure story.

4. Select a point of view to use—first person or third person.

5. Plan story events.
   There must be an obstacle to overcome.
   There must be fast-moving action.
      a. What will happen?
      b. What will the climax be?
      c. How will the story end?

6. Outline the basic information.
   Include clues leading to the treasure, secret, or new land.
      a. Beginning—Establish the characters and setting.
      b. Middle—Describe events, including the climax.
      c. End—Plan how the story will end.

7. Write your story.

# Write a Fantasy Story

1. Where is your story going to begin?

2. Name and describe story characters.
   Are you going to have animals or objects that act like people in your story?

3. Describe the time and location of the setting.
   Remember, the setting may change if characters move between the real and imaginary worlds.

4. Select a point of view to use—first person or third person.

5. Plan story events.
   a. What will happen?
   b. What will the climax be?
   c. How will the story end?

6. Outline the basic information.
   a. Beginning—Establish the characters and setting.
   b. Middle—Describe events, including the climax.
   c. End—Plan how the story will end.

7. Write your story.

# Write Science Fiction

1. Where is your story going to begin?
   The story can occur on Earth in the future, on another planet, aboard a spaceship, or on a space station.

2. Name and describe story characters.
   Characters can be humans, aliens, or unusual characters such as robots or computers.

3. Describe the time and location of the setting.

4. Select a point of view to use—first person or third person.

5. Plan story events.
   Remember, whatever equipment or means of transportation used in the story must be based on real science.
   a. What will happen?
   b. What will the climax be?
   c. How will the story end?

6. Outline the basic information.
   a. Beginning—Establish the characters and setting.
   b. Middle—Describe events, including the climax.
   c. End—Plan how the story will end.

7. Write your story.

# Evan-Moor's
# 10 Best-Selling
# WRITING TITLES

### How to Write a Story, Grades 1–3

Four step-by-step writing units help young writers create sensible stories with a beginning, a middle, and an end. Includes a story-writing center with reproducible charts, prompts, and writing forms. 96 pages.
**Correlated to current standards.**
Grades 1–3    EMC 799

### How to Write a Story, Grades 4–6

Includes lessons and reproducibles to help students learn the parts of a story, reproducible planning forms, and guidelines for writing in six different genres. Includes a story-writing center with reproducible charts, prompts, and writing forms. 96 pages.
**Correlated to current standards.**
Grades 4–6    EMC 794

### Writing Poetry with Children

A step-by-step guide for teaching students to write couplets, cinquains, haiku, and limericks. Includes reproducible instructions and illustrated writing forms. 96 pages.
**Correlated to current standards.**
Grades 1–6    EMC 734

### Poetry Patterns & Themes

Includes lessons and reproducible forms for 41 types of poetry, including couplets, haiku, limericks, and recipe poetry. 96 pages.
**Correlated to current standards.**
Grades 3–6    EMC 733

### Write a Super Sentence

Through 15 step-by-step guided lessons, students brainstorm adjectives, nouns, verbs, and where-and-when phrases, and use them to expand a simple sentence. Includes reproducible student activity pages and a writing center. 64 pages.
**Correlated to current standards.**
Grades 1–3    EMC 205

### Paragraph Writing

Includes teaching ideas, reproducible forms, and a paragraph-writing center. Topics include parts of a paragraph, types of paragraphs, and planning paragraphs. 80 pages.
**Correlated to current standards.**
Grades 2–4    EMC 246

### Writing Fabulous Sentences & Paragraphs

Lessons and activities progress from writing sentences to writing paragraphs. Complete teacher instructions and over 70 reproducible models and student writing forms. Includes an answer key. 112 pages.
**Correlated to current standards.**
Grades 4–6    EMC 575

### Giant Write Every Day—Daily Writing Prompts

300 "Quickwrites"—25 topics each month for short, daily practice; 202 story starters and titles for longer, more formal writings; 141 reproducible writing forms. 12 monthly sections. 176 pages.
**Correlated to current standards.**
Grades 2–6    EMC 775

### Writing Forms—Tops & Bottoms

Students will be motivated to do their best work when you showcase their reports, stories, or handwriting, by putting their papers in the middle of these two-piece forms. 160 pages.
Grades K–2    EMC 596

### Creative Writing Ideas

Activities include draw and write, riddles, sequence and write, letter writing, and more! 96 pages.
Grades 2–4    EMC 206